In the darkness of the night is where we find life.

CAST

By Rowan Aderyn

To my wonderful husband, who saved me from the night.

My children, who brought light into my life.

Every friend who ever helped show me the path, and my therapist, who guided me on a journey through the past.

I dedicate this book of poems to you.

You have all helped me in more ways than words can say. You have supported me, encouraged me, and believed in me, even when I didn't believe in myself. You have helped me to heal, to grow, and to find my voice.

I am so grateful for each and every one of you. Thank you for being there for me, always.

With love and gratitude always, Row

Introduction

The poems in this anthology are a journey through the life of a survivor of trauma. Born into a world of abuse and violence, the author has faced unimaginable challenges. The poems in this collection are raw, honest, and unflinching. They explore the darkest corners of the human experience, but they also offer hope. The author's journey is one of survival and transformation. They have emerged from the depths of trauma to find a life filled with love, meaning, and purpose.

The anthology explores a variety of themes related to trauma, including,

- Abuse
- Identity
- Healing
- Resilience
- Hope

The author's poems are a powerful exploration of the impact of trauma on the human psyche. They offer a unique and personal perspective on the journey of healing and recovery. The anthology raises awareness of the many challenges faced by survivors of trauma. The author's journey is a testament to the power of the human spirit to heal and overcome adversity.

From Row

In this anthology, I explore my journey as a survivor of childhood abuse. I write about the darkness, the pain, the fear. But I also write about the hope, the resilience, and the love that carried me through.

I write for my childhood self, the one who stood alone in the shadows, wondering if they would ever be okay. I write for all the other survivors who are still fighting, still hoping, still dreaming. I write to tell you that we are not alone, and as long as the future is yet to be written, hope is never lost.

The Real Introduction

To Row,

I am sorry for all the times I stood by, for every occasion I failed to act, for silencing your voice and turning all that hatred inward.

I know for a long time you believed I should have done more. I should have fought back. I should have protected you, shielded you from the darkness. But I was so scared, so small, so alone. And though time meant I grew up, I was still really that scared child, trapped in a world of possibilities.

The truth is I did fight for you every day. We may not have fought back, but we fought forward. We poured all our energy into hope, into carving out the person we wanted to be. Into gathering every ounce of kindness and finding every speck of joy. We let every lesson teach us and we stored that wisdom until we could step into the light.

The day is coming when you find something worth fighting for. When you find the courage to say 'enough' and step into the unknown. And it's worth it. All our dreams come true, we find our house upon a hill and fill it with love. We build that home where joy seeps into the walls. And it is better than we ever hoped for.

You were right to fight for hope. Hold on to that.
Row

Table of Contents: Cast

I Am Sorry

I am sorry that I made you stand again.
When all you wanted to do was stay against the floor.
To let the world around you stop.
To fall through a moment that never ended, alone.
I made you face the next torment in the hope of a reprieve.

I am sorry I didn't fight back.
I forced the fight inward.
I took the power from your fists.
I told you there was a better way and I never found it.
I built you a world to escape to, but you could never truly hide.

I am sorry I didn't get you out.
I looked towards the horizon and told you the dream was
enough.
I made you stay, let you believe the fear of the unknown mattered
more than the familiarity of your pain.

I am sorry I couldn't stop it.
That I never held the power to make that be the last.
That you had to force your way forward.

I am sorry that I silenced you.
That my words were led by fear.
That in every silent scream there was no one there to hear.

Breathe

I try to inhale, but nothing arrives.

I grasp at my mouth wondering why.

The air it has left me.

The light slips away.

Darkness inhales me.

I am bound for the grave.

Alone

You won't find me.
I am lost to the silence of nothing.
An illusion of what I could have been.

You can try to drag me back to reality, and for a while perhaps you'll win.
Triumphant you will turn your back and I will fade once more.

I know you feel frustrated when your efforts are in vain.
You don't understand how emptiness can be so consuming.
How when the battle is won it is lost.
For as long as there is a fight to win, the cost shall be the peace within.

Would you expect a blind man to see because you turned up the lights?
Or a lame man to walk because you slowed down the treadmill?
Why do you expect me to be happy when I am without the ability to feel?
Why do you want me to smell the roses when I cannot even breathe?

Tell me a thousand times how lucky I am.
Tell me that the world is a vast and beautiful place.
List the reasons I should be grateful.
And the joy that fills this space.

The journey down was hard as I resisted the decline.

Clawing into every moment as the darkness stole my life.

But here at the bottom the pain has somehow drifted.
The words no longer cut me.
There is no fight.
No desperation for the light.
There is a peace here, alone in the dark.

Perhaps you should just leave me here.

Memories

Memories spark unrequested.

Igniting every sense.

Suffocating life.

Dragging me from this time to a place I once had been.

Stealing possibility.

Trapping me in history.

Home

You expect me to be happy, to celebrate and smile.
I paint the joy across my face whilst underneath I hide.

I understand you're here now, and for you that is enough.
But all I see is darkness, in the forcing of your love.

A part of me wishes that the promise of your dream.
Would be enough to make it true, enough to set you free.

But those never-ending nightmares will always find their way.
To drown out all the happiness and suffocate our days.

I would be foolish to resolve myself to the safety of your hope.
So silently I hold the line and of my dreams let go.

Stolen

I watched you slip away, behind those steely eyes.
Dragged into that other place, where hope has gone to die.

I tried to be your life jacket, to hold you up for air.
But the murky depths they dragged you still, further to despair.

I had to let you slip away, into the depths unseen.
For if I held on one more moment, it would have taken me.

But as I watched you go my heart broke upon the shore.
If only love had been enough, I could have given more.

I am so sorry my strength failed to find a way.
A way to keep your head above the tide that stole your days.

Only You

I hate you for the futures stolen in the night.
I hate you for just standing still when you should have learnt to fight.

I hate you for the longing of a future not yet seen.
I hate you for the wishes cast into an empty dream.

I hate you for the kindness you begged others to express.
I hate you for knowing your worth was always less.

I hate you for the hope which you refused to relinquish.
I hate you for the fear you failed to extinguish.

I hate the way you kept your head above the tide.
I hate you for every tear that you failed to cry.

I hate you for the strength you showed when everything was lost.
If you had simply broken then it may not have been at such a cost.

Hold Back the Tide

Don't open yourself to the ink which bleeds across your skin.
You can wash it from your flesh if you never let it in.

Darkness

You dragged me to the darkness and held me in that place.
No amount of wishing would allow me to escape.
Your grip was tighter than my arms it bore into my soul.
The more I fought to free myself the less you would let go.

And so, I chose the only route and to the darkness I succumb.
I let myself fall ever deeper, my mind and soul both numb.

But with my final gasping breath I made a desperate plea.
That whilst the darkness stole my days it never would claim me.
To hold that truth of who I was softly in my core.
So when the nightmare ended, I could find myself once more.

This Coat

This heavy coat of shame, I wear with growing weight,
Crafted by their hands from torture and from hate.

I wish I could discard it, and leave it long behind.
But it's sewn into my flesh, and cannot be set aside.

I've tried to shake it off, I've picked along the seams.
But every time I try, the thread just runs more deep.

Perhaps I am afraid, that if I tear it from my soul,
The flesh that it will take with it, will mean I'm never whole.

With every growing lesson, I have built with it my strength.
This coat is now my armour, and without it I am spent.

Fortress

I fought for you with every moment, with tooth, and bone, and blood.
I fought with every word and breath, beyond the realms of love.

I stepped into the fray, without knowing what may be.
I only wished to save you from the nightmares which broke me.

I would fight whilst blood ran quickly, and breath was held in hostage.
I would fight with every ounce of me without asking what the cost is.

I would force myself to guard you.
From the threat of everything.
And in doing so I stole your life.
For nothing could get in.

No darkness could consume you, nor light could break those walls.

The fortress I had built for you did more than it intended.
It saved you from the pain of life and in that, your life ended.

Back Against the Door

Back firmly on the door, feet braced against the floor.
Holding your breath with every creak, every whispered groan of
the world settling into sleep, taunting you or warning you to stay
awake, stay awake.

Your watch has just begun, and you are already spent.
Digging for the strength to hold open cement cast eyelids.
As energy seeps from you and spills onto the floor.
Imagination buffered by the fear of reality.
Calculating options for exit or defence.
A maze of probabilities, mapless and divided.
As time drags by eliciting every ounce of its worth.

Drawing on all within reach.
As if grasping at morning will bring it closer.
Head bobbing, body jerking, fitted sleep drags you under, casting
doubt on your hope.
Trapped and defenceless with no escape, no option but to sit with
your back against the door.

Breath held for an eternity with the passing of night.
Just make it to morning, through the darkness to the light.

The Battle Unseen

I worried you'd consume me, if I released you from your cage.
Your strength would overpower me, and I could not run away.

As the key clicked into place, and the gate swung open wide,
I braced myself for impact, to defend the soul inside.

Frozen in that moment, waiting to succumb.
Hiding from the fear, that my life would be undone.

But as the memories faded, and drifted to the past.
I believed the threat you posed was nothing more than that.

I walked away with confidence, defences washed away.
Gave the guard some time off, with no need for him to stay.

But now I sense my lesson is drawing in quite fast.
You were never going to pounce on me, but you're closing in at last.

I feel your stalking presence, growing stronger every day.
I want to call the guard back, but he's left this barren place.

I'll muster new defences, raise a new attack.
I won't wait for you to find me, I'll never turn my back.

I will fight until my last breath, until the war is won.
But what happens when I beat you, and find it's me I've overcome?

One More Drink

I understand it did much more than soak into your flesh.

It eroded your humanity.
Hollowed out your soul.
That one more drink was poison.
To any goodness you might hold.

What remained was not a man.
But a puppet to the dark.
Tarred by every drop you took.
Its venom left its mark.

I wish that fight was yours to win, that you could have given more.
With every sip you chose to take, you chose my pain over yours.

Desperation

Cut me deep and take away the pain.

If Only

If paper could hold all the fear I feel.

I would bleed into its pages until the ink ran dry.

For the words which find their roots release me from this cage.

This cage that once was home, this pen I once called life.

I Am Here

I am here though you can't see me.
The darkness all but hides my truth.
In the quiet confines of my mind.
Frozen in isolation, paralysed by fear.

I silently sit and watch the day pass me by.
Through a screen of my imagining.
A break from reality.
A shroud of protection.
Don't assume what you see is all that I am.
I sit behind the veil.
I wait for the moment the world is safe.

And if that moment never arrives, I shall find sanctity in those
moments of joy which force their way to find me.

World of Silence

It is easier not to speak, the silence drips off my tongue.
I consume your words and fail to find their place.

It is easier to fade into the safety of emptiness.
To rest beyond the grasp of the day.

It is easier to wait, for the answers won't appear.
When the questions are stolen from a world steeped in fear.

A Life Lived in Paper

We lived our lives, in ink, and paper.
In letters, frozen in time.
The words which spilled from our hearts, unbound by the fear of
our voices.
The freedom of a pen, enabling truth to pour out.

We cast ourselves into those pages.
Our hopes, our fears, our dreams.
I found you in those whispers, and knew then, what it was, to be
seen.

Talk Your Way to Freedom

How can I find the beauty in my pain?
Will you wash away the hurt, transform my disdain?

Do you hold the power to set my heart free?
Release me from that torment of impossibility.

How will I find justice, is it hidden in your mind?
Must I let you in, to release the soul inside?

Help

It's that word I dread to say,
though I'm crumbling away.

I clench my jaw shut tight,
and endure this endless night.

My stand against the tide,
though I slowly fade inside.

If my weakness wins the day,
I will surely lose my way.

Not a hope to find the path,
I shall be lost within the dark.

I must try to carry on,
Or I shall find myself, undone.

Just Breathe

Just breathe, I tell myself.
This feeling will pass.

Just breathe, I tell myself.
This feeling won't last.

Just breathe, I tell myself.
Just let it fade away.

Just breathe, I tell myself.
Tomorrow's a new day.

I See You

I see you swallowed by the darkness.
Succumbing to its weight.
Dragged under by its current.
Left broken in its wake.

I see you lock away your heart.
In the hope you can be free.
Free from all the voices.
That refuse to let you be.

I see you hollow, burnt to ash.
Silenced by life's lies.
But in your mind you find yourself,
as a Phoenix free to fly.

Awoken

I lie awake in bed, schooling myself to breathe.
Coaching each inhalation, desperate for reprieve.

A constant state of panic, aware of every twitch.
Over-tuned into my body, with its riving, high strung pitch.

I repeat my broken mantra, everything is fine.
But I know the truth is far from that, I'm running out of time.

What I would give for just a moment of that peace I used to know.
To wake without anxiety, to breathe, and then let go.

More Than I Am

You can take my innocence stolen in that slow decline.

You can twist my words to fit your own design.

You can extinguish my hope and suffocate my dreams.

You can drive fear into my heart and take love away from me.

You can steal what you wish of my hard fought joy.

Darken each day to night and night to starless sky.

These things may be your prize, but you never will take me.

For I am more than memories, I am endless possibility.

I Don't Want to Know

Don't tell me my salvation is there,
hidden in the dark.
If I must succumb to find it,
then let it be lost to me.

I don't want to hear that happiness is buried in the depths of my
despair.
The tides I have to reason with are more than I can bear.

Perhaps the darkness won't consume me.
Maybe if I bathe in its icy waters it will dissipate in its persistence
to be felt.

But if I drift out with the tide.
Surely the journey back will be too far.

Hold On. Let Go.

I want to hold on to those moments, when love was all we knew.
I fiercely grasp those memories, that were pure, and warm, and
true.
I replay every second, so they might warm my aching heart.
Those tightly guarded moments, before life drove us apart.

And in my strong desire to hold on to my dreams, sometimes I
can fail to see, letting go is what I need.

To free myself of all those times pain splintered through my soul.
Escape the unseen darkness from that place I once called home.
Cast out and leave behind those days which store no hope.
Release myself from torment, untie that guilt bound rope.

So, heart and mind, I know it's hard, these contradicting needs.
Keep hold of all the good times and from the bad let me be free.

Possibility

Sometimes the light only makes the darkness that much deeper.

The offer of hope makes its absence more known.

The silence in a room can deafen me.

And your presence in my life only makes me feel more alone.

I just have to hold onto that chance, however slim.

That the world still holds a future, where my life might still begin.

No Rescue

There is no one coming to rescue you.

No words which can save you from the fear of breaking free.

No shining knight to steal you from this place.

There is no happy ending except the one which you create.

No saviour who has kept a happy day for your pain.

Only the possibility of hope, and a step you can take.

Fight back, or fight forward, that is the decision you must make.

Behind Those Eyes

A flicker of hope,
in a glimmer of light.
A resilient star,
that shines in the night.

A ray of burning light, that cuts through the dark.
Proving without darkness, we can't see who we are.

Belonging

I never really fitted, in that group at school.
The ones who owned the yard, and thought they were so cool.

I never really fitted, in the dancing club.
My two left feet determined to simply trip me up.

I didn't make my A levels, I jumped that hostile ship.
So pupil of the year was certainly not it.

Even in my home, I never fitted there,
I had to find a new one, one which sort of cared.

My place was never clear to me, it never felt just right.
That sense of belonging was always hidden from my sight.

But in all of my attempts, in searching to belong,
I never really realised I was getting it all wrong.

So I thought I'd try a different tack and stopped trying to fit in.
I stopped looking to the outside and started looking in.

Free from all the measures of a world I did not make.
A chance to build my own world, to explore and to create.

Who Am I?

Who am I?

But an echo of fate yet struck.

A muddle of loss and hope.

A dance yet spun.

Or die yet cast.

Am I anything or everything until I am nothing?

Is it not only then that my story is written that I can be defined?

From moment to moment my focus evolves, my perspective always anew.

My heart sings to me, its melody ever changing, a song yet sung surely cannot be wrote.

I can be everything and nothing, every decision a chance to renew, every lesson an opportunity to try again.

I am not defined by what they see or what I believe.

I am only defined by the limits of possibility.

I Feel a Change

I feel that promised movement.
A whisper on a breeze.
For the winter has been long and my hopes shredded in its rage.

But there is a warmth that echoes in the softness of the morning,
bringing with it a promise, a chance to start anew.
To tear my roots from their bed and find a new home.

To let my dreams sink into fertile ground and watch them bloom.

Let's hope tomorrow beds in deep, anchors in every nook.
And brings with it the possibility that yesterday once took.

Wonder

I wonder what you'll give to me.
What time you will bestow.

What wonders will reveal themselves.
In a world I think I know.

Every day unlike the last yet set against them all.

Scribe this story yet to cast the writing on the wall.

Lead me to my heart's surrender, let the day unfold.
Take me on this journey through a tale that's yet been told.

Hope

There is hope in that longing to hold you.
In those moments you create.
Your presence like a melody holds me in this place.
The anticipation of your gentle words, shaped only by your love.
And the softness of your touch, its magic cast in silent knowing.

There is hope in the morning for a day yet written and unknown.
My unspoken companion, that hope I long to hold.

There is hope in the wishes I cast, heard only by the stars.
I hope I might be worthy of your tender loving heart.

When I'm gone, I hope that love remains.

Speak and I Will Listen

Envelop me in words.
Let me sink into your mind.

Take me from this place.
And pause the hands of time.

Show me all you see.
Teach me all you know.

Take me from this moment.
So my life might now unfold.

Hold On

I know you're there, but I can't quite see.
The darkness has all but consumed me.

I feel your presence, in that far-off place.
I long to bask in your embrace.

I hold my breath, in sweet anticipation,
aching for your awaited revelation.

I pray I'm worthy of your grace.
That you'll find my soul, in this barren place.

I know you're there and I hope one day,
hope will drive the darkness away.

Hear Me, See Me

My words fall like silence, cast across an endless night.
Their meaning and intent failing to elicit their design.

Not heard, or received, or consumed, or understood.
Just echoed back towards my soul.
Cast aside from their lack of worth.

How can I find the right cipher to unlock your heart?

It is not money, nor fame nor gifts that I desire.
It is simply to be heard.
Don't you know the power your silence contains, the gift that
your ears can offer?

Not to correct, or reshape, or destroy my speech, but to offer it a
refuge.
A place those words can land, a place where they can rest.

For everybody's truth deserves a home.

Find Me

Find me beyond the sunrise, in those moments yet to be.
Hold me in that instant, of simple possibility.

In that light that's yet to reach us, to throw shadow into shade.
Take me in your knowing, and hold me in that place.

Found

You found me, in the darkness.
You dragged me to the light.
You fought away the monsters which haunted me at night.

You found me in the chaos.
You silenced all the pain.
You brought about a peace in me that let me start again.

Searching

That tiny spark ignited in us, cast from the cosmos into life.

If we are brave enough to seek our purpose, surely it is simply to be the keeper of that light.

To search for the moments which build our fire.
To hold it in our knowing.
To nurture its desire.

Each passion carefully crafted uniquely for your soul.
And so, we should seek that which makes us whole.

How often do we confer with that ember, that tiny spark which speaks.
Of desires and dreams and limits and needs.
If we master its song and protect it from the storm, surely we shall find a raging fire within us all.

Wanting

I want to know the world like you do.
Every facet of the day.
I want to feel the highs and lows, to dance within their grace.

I want to know my being, every wrinkle of its skin.
To hold every part of me with love, and know the soul within.

I want to smell the roses, and the ripples they unfold.
To share with you a story of a past that's yet untold.

To unwind all the chaos I have held against the door.
To let my broken soul spool onto the floor.
Then dip into its edges a brush or palette knife, and paint a new
design, that redefines my life.

More Than Words

You found me in the darkness.
You dragged me to the light.

You fought away the monsters that haunted me at night.

You found me in the chaos, you silenced all the screams.
You brought about a peace in me where my soul might now step in.

You gave me so much more than the measure of your time.
You gave me joy and let love in, you simply saved my life.

Love

For every moment you give to me.

You capture another piece of my heart.

I keep believing you have already enthralled it all, but you always find more.

Cast

I am not broken, I am whole.
A single person yet to unfold.
Courageous in fear, hopeful in the dark.
Beautiful and ugly, gentle, and stark.

Woven in time, a tapestry of life.
A melody unsung, the words yet to write.
I don't need mending. I am not undone.
I am all I will yet become.

Forged in fire and bathed in the night.
Perfect imperfection.
Cast into life.

The words we find hidden in possibility, can often be the thing which sets us free.

About the Author

Rowan Aderyn is an award-winning change maker who has a passion for storytelling and writing. They were born in Wales and after experiencing years of abuse at home spent a number of years in foster care before returning to the same abusive home where they were thrown back into unimaginable trauma.

Following a harrowing first couple of decades of life, they established themselves in a new home with their little sister and continued to grow from strength to strength. They have had a hugely successful career delivering change in the financial services sector and working as a guest and part time lecturer. They have been happily married for over fifteen years and have two wonderful children.

In more recent years Rowan has begun to find their voice and is taking action to use their skills and experience as a force for good. Establishing a charity for people who have experienced the care system, regularly speaking on the topics of mental health, gender, and inclusion.

They are passionate about using their writing to raise awareness of mental health issues and to empower others who have experienced trauma to find their own voice.

Their work is known for its lyrical beauty, its emotional depth, and its exploration of themes such as love, trauma, and identity. Rowan's poetry is deeply personal, yet it also resonates with readers on a universal level. Their writing tackles difficult subjects in an honest and accessible way, whilst giving space for the reader's own perspective. Their poems are full of rich emotion and thought-provoking insights. Their work is both moving and inspiring, and it is sure to leave a lasting impact on readers.

Printed in Great Britain
by Amazon

31975810R10037